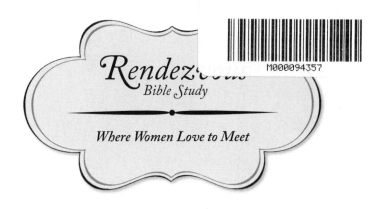

Rendezvous
Bible Study

Where Women Love to Meet

by Laura Greiner & Sharon Kohring

Joy Ride  Philippians

Personal Guidebook for Bible Study

Group

Incredible things will happen™

www.group.com

Rendezvous Joy Ride: Philippians
Personal Guidebook for Bible Study
Copyright © 2007 Group Publishing, Inc.

Visit our Web site: **www.group.com**

Credits
Authors: Laura Ross Greiner and Sharon Y. Kohring
Editor/Project Manager: Amber Van Schooneveld
Senior Developer: Amy Nappa
Chief Creative Officer: Joani Schultz
Art Director: Andrea Filer
Book Designer and Cover Art Designer: Samantha Wranosky
Print Production Artist: Rebecca Finkel
Production Manager: DeAnne Lear

Unless otherwise indicated, all Scripture quotations are taken from the *Holy Bible,* New Living Translation, copyright © 1996, 2004. Used by permission of Tyndale House Publishers, Inc., Carol Stream, Illinois 60188. All rights reserved.

ISBN 978-0-7644-3511-9

10 9 8 7 6 5 4 3 2 1   16 15 14 13 12 11 10 09 08 07
Printed in the United States of America.

Contents

Introduction

Welcome to *Rendezvous: Joy Ride*!

We're so excited you've chosen to be a part of this unique Bible study with us.

Your *Personal Guidebook for Bible Study* is your ticket to join us on a joy ride! This *Rendezvous* study is all about learning and experiencing the joy God has for each of us. Through studying the book of Philippians— which is packed with Paul's expression of the joy we find in the Christian life—you'll learn how to embrace the joy of God each day. This Guidebook includes questions and activities you'll be doing with your group each week. The Nudge Questions will help nudge your heart closer to understanding the theme for each session. You'll be using this Guidebook at each session, so make sure you bring it with you.

This Guidebook will also help you deepen your relationship with God outside of group time. The "Rendezvous and Beyond" section and "Rendez-vous for Two" will give you personal enrichment ideas, thoughts for reflection, time to spend alone with God, and tools for digging deeper into the Bible.

We pray for you as you embark upon this *Joy Ride*! We pray specifi-cally that each ride would show you more of what God has for all of us—a life infused with his joy!

With joy,

Laura and Sharon

A Thankful Heart Is a Joyful Heart

Write down Philippians 1:3.

_____

_____

_____

_____

_____

Write down Philippians 4:6.

_____

_____

_____

_____

_____

Whom did you picture when you had your eyes closed?

_____

What was the first thing you thought about when you pictured that person?

_____

_____

_____

Nudge Questions

More, More, More

• When you're "blue," what do you tend to do? What healthy things do you do? What not-so-healthy things do you do?

• What is something you've coveted that belonged to someone else? Why do you think God included in the Ten Commandments "you must not covet your neighbor's house…or anything else that belongs to your neighbor" (Exodus 20:17)?

• In what ways do you struggle with being unsatisfied with what you have?

A-Z Thanks-Giver Ideas

a. Pray out loud to God with your thanks—audibly. Shout, even!

b. Play the piano as a way of expressing your thanks.

c. Sing songs of thanks.

d. Talk more to other people about how thankful you are.

e. Put a sign up in your kitchen that reads, "I give thanks to the Lord!"

f. Keep a journal of thanks.

g. Wear a thanksgiving bracelet or ring, and every time you look at it, give thanks to God.

h. Do a thank walk or a thank hike once a month. Thank God the entire time you're walking or hiking.

i. Do a word study on *thanksgiving* in the Bible, and copy down all the Scriptures on cards to keep in your purse (use www.biblegateway.com to conduct a quick search).

j. Start your morning and end your day with thanks; put a sign next to your bed as a reminder.

k. Give a thanks sacrifice…give up something as a token of gratitude between Thanksgiving and Christmas.

l. Visit a children's hospital or a nursing home to remind yourself of *all* you have to be thankful for.

m. Go around the dinner table on Sunday night and have each person take a turn sharing what he or she is thankful to God for.

n. Memorize a verse a month on being a thanks-giver.

o. Write God regular thank you notes and keep them in a box, pulling them out when you need a reminder of all he has done for you.

p. Write out what you are battling or struggling with in life, and then thank God that he is God, that he cares, that he's faithful, that he's trustworthy.

q. Put a thanksgiving memento in each room of your house.

r. Create your own symbol for thanksgiving and sign your letters with it; use this symbol anyplace you'd sign your name.

s. Make a CD with only thanksgiving worship music, and listen to it at least once a week.

t. Start a tradition at Christmas time to make the season more about the *Giver* than the gifts.

u. Watch *Veggie Tales: Madame Blueberry* with a few kids.

v. Write a letter to God on your birthday every year thanking him for what he did that year.

w. When you take a shower, make it a time of thanksgiving (after all, a hot shower is something to be very thankful for!).

x. When you're really struggling with someone, instead of praying for God to change the situation or person, spend time just giving thanks to God…say thanks for anything about the situation that you can find to be thankful for and give thanks that he's in control.

y. If you drive to the same place every day, choose a certain stretch of the drive to be completely devoted to thanksgiving each day.

z. Bake a cake and throw a "Thankful Party," inviting a few close friends over to celebrate all you are thankful for.

Trace your hand onto this page, and write in each finger one of the A-Z Thanks-Giver Ideas you will do (or come up with your own)!

Thanksgiving Ribbon Reminders

Blue Ribbon: _____

Green Ribbon: _____

Purple Ribbon: _____

Rendezvous and Beyond 🚲🚲

Use these ideas to keep growing in thankfulness in the following week.
  • Time yourself for one minute and write down everything that pops into your mind that you are thankful for.

_____

_____

_____

_____

_____

_____

_____

_____

_____

_____

_____

_____

_____

_____

_____

_____

_____

_____

_____

_____

Look over your list. What's at the top of it? Read James 1:17, and review your list again.

> "Whatever is good and perfect comes down to us from God our Father, who created all the lights in the heavens. He never changes or casts a shifting shadow." ☞ James 1:17

• Reread the "A-Z Thanks-Giver Ideas" list. Circle the one you want to implement most in your life (or write out your own!). Think of a close friend you could ask to keep you accountable for doing this, and write down her name. Ask your friend to specifically check in with you once a month (or so) just to ask how your thanksgiving commitment is going.

Friend's name: _____

Thanksgiving habit you want her to hold you accountable for:

_____

_____

• Try to thank God every night before you go to bed this week for everything he did for you during the day. Give particular attention to thanking him for the small stuff that you may normally not even think about (a good conversation you may have had, a hug from your child, your pillow, and so on).

• Read Colossians 2:7.

> "Let your roots grow down into him, and let your lives be built on him. Then your faith will grow strong in the truth you were taught, and you will overflow with thankfulness." ☞ Colossians 2:7

Why do you think as we grow closer to God and our faith grows stronger, we'll overflow with thankfulness? What's the connection?

_____

_____

_____

_____

_____

• Often we thank God for what he has done, but it's important to also thank him for who he is. I (Laura) know when someone thanks me for something I've done, it feels good, but what feels even better is when I'm thanked for who I am. For instance, if my friend thanks me for doing her a favor, that feels good. But if my friend tells me I'm a great friend and goes on to say what she appreciates about my character, that feels even better! God loves to be thanked for *who* he is, too. Write out 10 attributes of God, and then spend time appreciating and thanking him for those qualities.

1. _____

2. _____

3. _____

4. _____

5. _____

6. _____

7. _____

8. _____

9. _____

10. _____

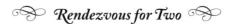

❧ *Rendezvous for Two* ❧

Have a rendezvous with God, just the two of you.

> "The Lord is my strength and shield. I trust him with all my heart. He helps me, and my heart is filled with joy. I burst out in songs of thanksgiving." ☞ Psalm 28:7

Spend time meditating on this verse and bursting with thankfulness. Write here any thoughts you're struck with during this time.

_____

_____

_____

_____

_____

_____

_____

_____

_____

_____

_____

_____

_____

_____

Joy, Certainly!

Discuss: What is the opposite of confidence?

> The original Greek word used for "certain" in this verse carried the idea of being persuaded, as in "I didn't always feel this way but now, because of
>
> _____
>
> [some event], I am now persuaded. I am now convinced. I have no doubt."

Meanwhile, Saul was uttering threats with every breath and was eager to kill the Lord's followers. So he went to the high priest. He requested letters addressed to the synagogues in Damascus, asking for their cooperation in the arrest of any followers of the Way he found there. He wanted to bring them—both men and women—back to Jerusalem in chains.

As he was approaching Damascus on this mission, a light from heaven suddenly shone down around him. He fell to the ground and heard a voice saying to him, "Saul! Saul! Why are you persecuting me?"

"Who are you, lord?" Saul asked. And the voice replied, "I am Jesus, the one you are persecuting! Now get up and go into the city, and you will be told what you must do."

The men with Saul stood speechless, for they heard the sound of someone's voice but saw no one! Saul picked himself

up off the ground, but when he opened his eyes he was blind. So his companions led him by the hand to Damascus. He remained there blind for three days and did not eat or drink.

Now there was a believer in Damascus named Ananias. The Lord spoke to him in a vision, calling, "Ananias!" "Yes, Lord!" he replied. The Lord said, "Go over to Straight Street, to the house of Judas. When you get there, ask for a man from Tarsus named Saul. He is praying to me right now. I have shown him a vision of a man named Ananias coming in and laying hands on him so he can see again."

"But Lord," exclaimed Ananias, "I've heard many people talk about the terrible things this man has done to the believers in Jerusalem! And he is authorized by the leading priests to arrest everyone who calls upon your name." But the Lord said, "Go, for Saul is my chosen instrument to take my message to the Gentiles and to kings, as well as to the people of Israel. And I will show him how much he must suffer for my name's sake."

So Ananias went and found Saul. He laid his hands on him and said, "Brother Saul, the Lord Jesus, who appeared to you on the road, has sent me so that you might regain your sight and be filled with the Holy Spirit." Instantly something like scales fell from Saul's eyes, and he regained his sight. Then he got up and was baptized. Afterward he ate some food and regained his strength.

Saul stayed with the believers in Damascus for a few days. And immediately he began preaching about Jesus in the synagogues, saying, "He is indeed the Son of God!" All who heard him were amazed. "Isn't this the same man who caused such devastation among Jesus' followers in Jerusalem?" they asked. "And didn't he come here to arrest them and take them in chains to the leading priests?" ☞ Acts 9:1-21

Discuss and write down a few key points of the Saul-to-Paul story.

_____

_____

_____

• Why was Paul so bold about God's abilities and faithfulness?

• Write one thing you've placed your confidence in that's failed you.

Nudge Questions

Confidence

Read Psalm 34:1-3.

> "I will praise the Lord at all times. I will constantly speak his praises. I will boast only in the Lord; let all who are helpless take heart. Come, let us tell of the Lord's greatness; let us exalt his name together." Psalm 34:1-3

• Boast together about the Lord by sharing some ways God has been faithful in his care for you.

• Why is it so easy to climb out of the rowboat (focused on God) and back into a canoe (focused on all the worries and troubles that lay ahead)?

• As we row the boat of life, we need to fix our eyes on him and his faithfulness in our past. How can we help each other stay in the rowboat?

• Partner up and choose one way to follow-up with your partner this week. Below, write down that idea and your partner's name as a reminder.

What are you going to do this week to help your partner "stay in the rowboat"?

_____

_____

_____

What are some things that might help you commit to climb into God's rowboat and put your confidence in him?

_____

_____

_____

_____

_____

_____

_____

_____

Rendezvous and Beyond ⊛⊛

Use these ideas to keep growing your confidence in God in the following week.
    • Everyday this week, reread the words you wrote under the rowboat to remind yourself to make the choice to trust in God, not in your own efforts or strength.

    • Read the following passage everyday this week.

This is what the Lord says:
"Cursed are those who put their trust in mere humans,
    who rely on human strength
    and turn their hearts away from the Lord.
They are like stunted shrubs in the desert,
    with no hope for the future.
They will live in the barren wilderness,
    in an uninhabited salty land.
But blessed are those who trust in the Lord
    and have made the Lord their hope and confidence.
They are like trees planted along a riverbank,
    with roots that reach deep into the water.
Such trees are not bothered by the heat
    or worried by long months of drought.
Their leaves stay green,
    and they never stop producing fruit."
    ☞ Jeremiah 17:5-8

    • As you go through your week, make mental notes when you see dried, stunted plants as compared to green, healthy plants. Meditate on the contrast between those who "trust in mere humans" and those who "trust in the Lord."

    • Take a field trip to a botanical garden this week or go on a hike. Spend time in the garden or on the hike talking to God about how he is your hope and confidence. Picture yourself as a growing tree planted on the river's edge—because you trust in him.

• Start a prayer journal, listing the date and prayer request. Leave space to enter an update and praise as you track the amazing ways God answers your prayers (with a "yes" or by profoundly changing your requests and attitude!). Remember, confidence in God is built as we *know* who we are putting our trust in!

• For more books on prayer, check out:
  Clinging: The Experience of Prayer by Emilie Griffin
  Prayer: Finding the Heart's True Home by Richard J. Foster
  Hearing God: Developing a Conversational Relationship with God
    by Dallas Willard

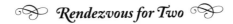

✑ *Rendezvous for Two* ✑

Have a rendezvous with God, just the two of you.

God wants us to come to him as we are, not as we think he wants us to be. You can be honest with God, you know. He knows you inside and out! Write out a prayer to God, expressing your difficulties in fully trusting him. Explain why it's so easy for you to trust in human strength. Ask God to help you believe him, giving you the strength you need to fully trust him each day.

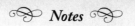 *Notes*

Joyfully Ever After

Write some things in the "Once Considered Valuable" column that you once regarded as really important. Then write in the "Now Considered Not Worth Much" column what you know isn't worth anything. For example, you might write in the "Once Considered Valuable" column "owning a big home," and in the "Now Considered Not Worth Much" column "gaining material things."

Add to this list as you think of additions throughout the week.

Once Considered Valuable	Now Considered Not Worth Much

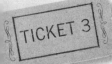
Things That Won't Last for Eternity

_____
_____
_____
_____
_____

Things That Matter for Eternity

_____
_____
_____
_____
_____

Nudge Questions

Ever After

• Pick someone to be your timer. In only one minute, list as many things
as possible in your life that have lasting, eternal value. Ready? Go!

_____
_____
_____
_____
_____

• Compare your lists.

• Why is it such a struggle to keep an eternal focus on life? What hinders you the most?

• What kinds of things have you done that have been helpful in maintaining an eternal focus? (Maybe spiritual disciplines such as silence, meditation, fasting; practical habits such as stopping to thank God for a flower that you walk past, and so on.) Develop a group list of practical ways you can nudge your minds toward an eternal focus.

_____

_____

_____

_____

_____

_____

_____

• In your group, find a prayer partner, and pray for each other this week, specifically in this area of eternal focus.

Partner's name: _____

Things to pray for your partner:

_____

_____

_____

_____

_____

Rendezvous and Beyond ⊗⊗

Use these ideas in the following week to help your perspective on your life match God's.

• On the Internet, go to Google Earth. Look up your address. There you are—your house! Now pull back to your neighborhood. Keep pulling back to your city, your country, your continent, the globe. Now *pause*. Contemplate the enormity of the world. Now do it again—look up your address and pull back. How do you feel? Small? Amazed? What else?

_____

_____

_____

_____

_____

_____

_____

_____

_____

_____

_____

_____

_____

_____

_____

_____

• Read Psalm 8 in all the following different Bible translations.

☞ **Psalm 8, New Living Translation**
O Lord, our Lord, your majestic name fills the earth!
Your glory is higher than the heavens.
You have taught children and infants
to tell of your strength,
silencing your enemies
and all who oppose you.

When I look at the night sky and see the work of your fingers
the moon and the stars you set in place
what are mere mortals that you should think about them,
human beings that you should care for them?
Yet you made them only a little lower than God
and crowned them with glory and honor.

You gave them charge of everything you made,
putting all things under their authority
the flocks and the herds
and all the wild animals,
the birds in the sky, the fish in the sea,
and everything that swims the ocean currents.

O Lord, our Lord, your majestic name fills the earth!

☞ **Psalm 8, The Message**
God, brilliant Lord,
Yours is a household name.
Nursing infants gurgle choruses about you;
Toddlers shout the songs
That drown out enemy talk,
And silence atheist babble.

I look up at your macro-skies, dark and enormous,
Your handmade sky-jewelry,
Moon and stars mounted in their settings.
Then I look at my micro-self and wonder,
Why do you bother with us?
Why take a second look our way?

Yet we've so narrowly missed being gods,
Bright with Eden's dawn light.
You put us in charge of your handcrafted world,
Repeated to us your Genesis-charge,
Made us lords of sheep and cattle,
Even animals out in the wild,
Birds flying and fish swimming,
Whales singing in the ocean deeps.

God, brilliant Lord,
Your name echoes around the world.

☞ Psalm 8, Contemporary English Version
Our Lord and Ruler,
your name is wonderful
everywhere on earth!
You let your glory be seen in the heavens above.
With praises from children
and from tiny infants,
you have built a fortress.
It makes your enemies silent,
and all who turn against you
are left speechless.
I often think of the heavens
your hands have made,
and of the moon and stars
you put in place.

Then I ask, "Why do you care
about us humans?
Why are you concerned
for us weaklings?"
You made us a little lower
than you yourself, and you have crowned us
with glory and honor.
You let us rule everything
your hands have made.
And you put all of it
under our power—
the sheep and the cattle,
and every wild animal,
the birds in the sky,
the fish in the sea,
and all ocean creatures.
Our Lord and Ruler,
your name is wonderful
everywhere on earth!

☞ **Psalm 8, King James Version**

O Lord, our Lord, how excellent is thy name in all the earth! who hast set thy glory above the heavens.

Out of the mouth of babes and sucklings hast thou ordained strength because of thine enemies, that thou mightest still the enemy and the avenger.

When I consider thy heavens, the work of thy fingers, the moon and the stars, which thou hast ordained;

What is man, that thou art mindful of him? and the son of man, that thou visitest him?

For thou hast made him a little lower than the angels, and hast crowned him with glory and honour.

Thou madest him to have dominion over the works of thy hands; thou hast put all things under his feet:

> All sheep and oxen, yea, and the beasts of the field;
> The fowl of the air, and the fish of the sea, and whatsoever passeth through the paths of the seas.
> O Lord our Lord, how excellent is thy name in all the earth!

• Now, write your own personal version of Psalm 8, inserting your name and naming things that create awe for you (in place of "what are mere mortals that you should think about them," put in your name).

_____

_____

_____

_____

_____

_____

_____

_____

_____

_____

_____

_____

_____

_____

_____

_____

_____

_____

_____

• If you haven't ever, memorize John 3:16. If you memorized it long ago, memorize it in another translation. One of the values of memorizing Scripture is that it allows you to reflect on it and meditate on it daily. Consider this: If you have trusted Jesus as your personal Savior, you, the real you, will not die but live eternally! *You* are eternal.

> "For God loved the world so much that he gave his one and only Son, so that everyone who believes in him will not perish but have eternal life." John 3:16

• Begin choosing to do one thing each week that could matter for eternity: Help someone in financial need; serve someone who is sick; pray for a friend who doesn't know Jesus as their Savior…Brainstorm a list right now of things you could do that could have long-term, even eternal implications:

_____

_____

_____

_____

_____

_____

_____

• Pray over the list you just wrote, and allow God to give you a passion to start with one of the things on your list *this very week*!

• Check out Eternal Perspective Ministries: www.epm.org or read these books:
> *Heaven* by Randy Alcorn
> *In Light of Eternity: Perspectives on Heaven* by Randy Alcorn

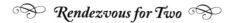

✑ *Rendezvous for Two* ✑

Have a rendezvous with God, just the two of you.

Spend at least five minutes each night before you go to sleep reviewing the spiritual realities of your day—the things that touched your life or that you did that will last for eternity. Record those things here:

- _____
- _____
- _____
- _____
- _____
- _____
- _____
- _____
- _____
- _____
- _____
- _____
- _____
- _____
- _____
- _____
- _____
- _____
- _____

At the end of the week, review all that you've written. Summarize any new thoughts you have on living with an eternal perspective.

❧ *Notes* ❧

 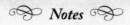

Multiply the Joy!

Qualities of a Great Friend

Studies show that the following traits are key to great friendships. Rate yourself from 1 to 10 on how well you think you're doing in each of these categories. (1 being "I really need to improve here" and 10 being "I think I got this one covered.")

Supportive	5
Encouraging	5
Dependable	4
Self-Disclosing	3
Spiritually Concerned	2
Trustworthy	7
Compassionate	7
Loyal	8
Honest	8

Search the Scriptures

Circle the word "you" and "your" every time they are listed in the verses below. Underline the words "my," "me," and "I."

☞ **Philippians 1:7-9; 4:1, 14-16, New Living Translation**

"So it is right that I should feel as I do about all of you, for you have a special place in my heart. You share with me the special favor of God, both in my imprisonment and in defending and confirming the truth of the Good News. God knows how much I love you and long for you with the tender compassion of Christ Jesus. I pray that your love will overflow more and more, and that you will keep on growing in knowledge and understanding."

"…Therefore, my dear brothers and sisters, stay true to the Lord. I love you and long to see you, dear friends, for you are my joy and the crown I receive for my work."

"…Even so, you have done well to share with me in my present difficulty. As you know, you Philippians were the only ones who gave me financial help when I first brought you the Good News and then traveled on from Macedonia. No other church did this. Even when I was in Thessalonica you sent help more than once."

☞ **Philippians 1:7-9; 4:14-16, The Message**

"It's not at all fanciful for me to think this way about you. My prayers and hopes have deep roots in reality. You have, after all, stuck with me all the way from the time I was thrown in jail, put on trial, and came out of it in one piece. All along you have experienced with me the most generous help from God. He knows how much I love and miss you these days. Sometimes I think I feel as strongly about you as Christ does!"

"… It was a beautiful thing that you came alongside me in my troubles…You Philippians well know, and you can be sure I'll never forget it, that when I first left Macedonia province, venturing out with the Message, not one church helped out in

the give-and-take of this work except you. You were the only one. Even while I was in Thessalonica, you helped out—and not only once, but twice."

Nudge Questions

Sharing Life

• Other than family members, who sticks with you through thick and thin? Think of one or two people. Pick one piece in your trail mix that represents this person. Tell your group how it represents them ("She's sweet like this dried cherry") and how they've stuck by you in the past.

• Paul showed us how "shared life" includes pouring into others as well as allowing others to pour into you. Which do you do better at— pouring into others or allowing others to pour into you? How so?

• Do you think Christian friendships should look different than other friendships? Why or why not?

• What is the biggest obstacle that gets in the way of vulnerably sharing your life with others? What steps can you take to remove that obstacle?

Friendship Ideas

1. Be intentional and committed; set a regular time and place to meet with a few friends who want to grow spiritually together. Make it a priority to be at the designated meeting times.
2. When you're together with close friends, be intentional in your conversation. Make sure each friend gets time to share what is going on in her heart and head. Get good at *listening* to each other.
3. Seek friends outside your stage of life. Find someone younger or older, with kids or without kids, working or staying at home; and then learn from each other!

4. Be a multi-tasker in your friendships, especially if your life is jam-packed and you can't find time to spend with friends. Do projects together once a month, such as painting bedrooms, reorganizing closets, cleaning cabinets, or exercising.

5. Pray together. Pray for each other. Find a prayer partner, and meet on a regular basis for prayer. Go on a regular prayer hike with friends. Pray together!

6. Go on weekend trips together. Going to a destination and spending multiple nights together is a great time to make memories and go deeper in friendship.

7. Learn to laugh together. A LOT! Life is so heavy that we need to turn it off sometimes and just laugh and be silly more often.

Shared Lives: Practical Applications

Write here some of the ideas you've brainstormed for sharing life together well.

1. _____

2. _____

3. _____

4. _____

5. _____

6. _____

7. _____

Circle your favorite idea and write here how you're going to put it into practice.

_____

_____

_____

_____

Rendezvous and Beyond

Use these ideas to grow your friendships this week.
  • Make a list of friends who are safe people in your life.

1. _____
2. _____
3. _____
4. _____
5. _____

  • What is it about these people that make them safe for you?

_____
_____
_____
_____
_____
_____
_____
_____

  • Make a list of friends who are unsafe people in your life. (Unsafe meaning you wouldn't feel comfortable being totally vulnerable with them.)

1. _____
2. _____
3. _____
4. _____
5. _____

• What is it about these people that make them unsafe?

_____

_____

_____

_____

_____

_____

• Do some soul searching. Are you a safe person for others? Ask God to show you one way you can improve as a friend to others. Write down whatever he puts on your heart.

_____

_____

_____

_____

_____

_____

_____

_____

_____

_____

_____

_____

_____

• Read the story below, and see which little girl you identify with more.

Madelyne and Jenna

Eight-year-old Jenna was playing school with her best friend, Madelyne, one afternoon when Madelyne informed her she couldn't have a sleepover that weekend because she had gotten in trouble.

"Why? What did you do?" asked Jenna.

"I don't want to tell you," Madelyne replied, looking down at the ground.

"Why not?"

"It's too embarrassing," Madelyne's cheeks flushed.

Jenna stopped playing and put her hands on her hips. "I tell you everything! You know all the bad stuff I've ever done!" Her lips drew into a tight knot. Madelyne burst into tears and ran to the office where her mom was going through paperwork.

After explaining what was going on, Madelyne cried some more. "I just can't tell her mom. It's too embarrassing."

Madelyne's mom wiped away her tears. "I know. Sometimes it's hard to tell other people things we've done that we're not proud of."

Jenna appeared in the kitchen doorway, her big blue eyes narrowed. "I have waited two years for this!" Jenna's voice rose as she spoke. "I have waited to be your trusted best friend. And now you won't even tell me this!"

Madelyne's mom put her hand on her daughter's shoulder. "Do you understand what Jenna is saying? She just wants you to trust her like she has trusted you."

"I just can't," squeaked Madelyne.

"You know, everyone has done things they are not proud of," Madelyne's mom continued.

"Really?" both girls said in unison, looking up at her. "What have you done?"

Madelyne's mom smiled and told the girls stories about embarrassing things she had done when she was a little girl. Her words seemed to give Madelyne the confidence she needed.

"OK," Madelyne swallowed. "I'll tell her." She took a big breath and then blurted out, "I lied."

Jenna stood there for a moment without a word. Finally she opened her mouth, "That's it? You lied?"

"MmHm," Madelyne nodded and looked down.

A huge smile lit up Jenna's face. "Good job, Madelyne! You told me!

You did it! Now let's celebrate."

Within a couple of minutes, Jenna had pulled out snacks, poured juice and written a sign that said, "Good Job Maddie Day!" The girls were still laughing and celebrating when Jenna's mom came to pick her up a short while later. After Jenna left, Madelyne looked at her mom with a new sparkle in her eyes. "I love her, mom."

"She's a good friend."

"And you know what, mom? Once I told her, it wasn't that hard."

"That's how it is when you share embarrassing stuff with a trusted friend." Madelyne smiled and skipped up the stairs to her room.

Which girl are you moe like: Maddie—scared to be vulnerable, or Jenna—ready to encourage, love, and support a hurting friend? Write here wich girl you relate ro move and why.

TICKET 4

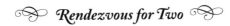

Rendezvous for Two

Have a rendezvous with God, just the two of you.

> "I no longer call you slaves, because a master doesn't confide
> in his slaves. Now you are my friends, since I have told you
> everything the Father told me." ☞ John 15:15

Read this verse and write down your reflections on what God is speaking to your heart and your life about friendship, community, and "shared life."

_____

_____

_____

_____

_____

_____

_____

_____

_____

_____

_____

_____

_____

_____

_____

_____

_____

_____

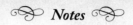 **Notes**

Joy Upside Down

Me First

Write the three characteristics of the "Me-First" lies on the triangle.

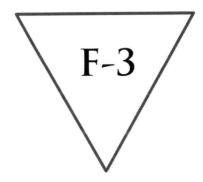

F-3

What Does God Say?

Read the verses below. Underline one verse or part of a verse that particularly stands out to you.

> "Then make me truly happy by agreeing wholeheartedly with each other, loving one another, and working together with one mind and purpose.
> Don't be selfish; don't try to impress others. Be humble, thinking of others as better than yourselves. Don't look out only for your own interests, but take an interest in others, too.

> You must have the same attitude that Christ Jesus had.
> Though he was God, he did not think of equality with God as
> something to cling to. Instead, he gave up his divine privileges;
> he took the humble position of a slave and was born as a human
> being. When he appeared in human form, he humbled himself
> in obedience to God and died a criminal's death on a cross."
> ☞ Philippians 2:2-8

Write down your thoughts and reflections about how the verse speaks to you personally.

Nudge Questions

Humility

• In Philippians 2:2-8 humility is referred to three different times. Find the verses that use the word *humble*, and read them together. What do you think Paul is trying to communicate to us regarding humility?

• In Matthew 11:29 Jesus says, *"Take my yoke upon you. Let me teach you, because I am humble and gentle at heart, and you will find rest for your souls."* In what ways do the life and teachings of Jesus on the topic of humility send us a very different message from our society? (Think about humility as it relates to people in Hollywood, professional sports, and politics.)

• God clearly states in the Bible that he is drawn to the humble. He's also clear that he opposes the proud. Think of your own life. Where do you struggle with pride? Are there similar struggles within your group?

• Martin Luther said, "God created the world out of nothing, and as long as we are nothing, He can make something out of us." What do you think this means? What does it look like to be "nothing?"

Timeline

Illustrate the timeline of your life. Mark different periods in your life when you were disobedient or held onto certain things you knew God wanted you to let go of.

Birth

Present

Nudge Questions

Holding On

• Share with each other about the levels of joy and peace in your life during the periods of disobedience on your timeline.

• Have someone in your group read John 15:10-11 out loud.

> "When you obey my commandments, you remain in my love, just as I obey my Father's commandments and remain in his love. I have told you these things so that you will be filled with my joy. Yes, your joy will overflow!" ☞ John 15:10-11

• Have you ever experienced the joy Jesus is talking about here? Describe what was going on in your life when you experienced it.

Rendezvous and Beyond ✿✿

Use these ideas to keep growing in obedience to God in the following week.

Several years ago I (Laura) was working on a writing project with another author. I never said it out loud, but I thought I was the better writer. Both my co-author and I were stunned when our editor had us rewrite the entire manuscript in a different style. That was hard. What was even harder was that I couldn't get the hang of the new style. My co-author got it right away. She whipped through rewriting her pieces while I was stuck writing and rewriting mine. After reading one of my many rewrites, our editor told me over the phone, "We're still not quite there yet." I hung up and cried.

I was humbled. I had been oblivious to the pride in my heart. My eyes were opened wide, and I saw my pride for what it was—sin. I'm so thankful for that humbling journey—it caused me to repent and turn to God anew.

• Pray for God to show you areas of your life where you might be blind to pride. Write some of those areas here.

_____

_____

_____

• In 2 Chronicles 7:14 God says, *"Then if my people who are called by my name will humble themselves and pray and seek my face and turn from their wicked ways, I will hear from heaven and will forgive their sins and restore their land."*

When I sought God's face, he did restore me (and my writing). Think about your own life. What area in your life needs to be restored? Spend time seeking God in this area. Give him total control of the reigns and confess any sins you may be holding on to.

_____

_____

_____

_____

_____

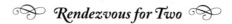

❧ *Rendezvous for Two* ❧

Have a rendezvous with God, just the two of you.

God yearns for us to remain in him. Close your eyes for a minute and picture him as the vine and you as one of his branches. Visualize yourself as being fed from the vine. Now picture yourself being cut off, broken off, no longer connected to the vine. Spend time journaling about the word *remain*. Remaining is an active, everyday choice. How does that play out in your life?

Joy Inside Out

Circle every time Paul writes "joy" or "rejoice" in the verses below.

> "But I will rejoice even if I lose my life, pouring it out like
> a liquid offering to God, just like your faithful service is an
> offering to God. And I want all of you to share that joy. Yes,
> you should rejoice, and I will share your joy."
> ☞ Philippians 2:17-20

Pouring Out Exercise

On the first row of cups below, write the names of people (or groups
of people) you pour your life into. (Use only one cup to list all of your
immediate family members.)

On the second row of cups, write the names of people who pour into
your life.

With a partner, discuss:
- Do you have more people who pour into your life or more people whom you pour into?

- What are your thoughts on the balance of pouring and receiving?

Nudge Questions

Servant

- What kinds of people in your life are easy for you to serve? Whom do you need to work at wanting to serve?

- Have someone read John 13:1-21. Jesus knew Judas was going to betray him, but he washed his feet. He humbly served Judas. Why? What was motivating Jesus to serve Judas?

- In what ways do you do a good job of serving others? How can you improve?

- Take some time and pray together as a group, asking God to help you become better servers.

Taking Genuine Interest Like Timothy

Who takes a genuine interest in your life, and how do they show this by their actions?

_____

_____

_____

Write down one idea someone shared for showing genuine interest in others that you'd like to try out.

_____

_____

_____

Write here how you, practically, are going to put this idea into action.

_____

_____

Follow Through Game

Game Rules

1. With your partner, find a common good intention you both have but haven't followed through on (such as visiting someone, helping someone, calling someone, saying you're sorry to someone, and so on).
2. Each of you write the good intention down at the "start" place in your own Guidebooks.
3. When the leader says, "Go" each player writes down next to the dots one reason she didn't get her "good intention" done. (This filled-in dot is called a "barrier." Examples of barriers are: too busy, stressed out, scared, forgetful, car broke down, and so on.)
4. When the Leader says "Stop," put down your pen. Count how many barriers you came up with.
5. The "winner" is the one who has the most barriers. Then complete the discussion that follows.

start

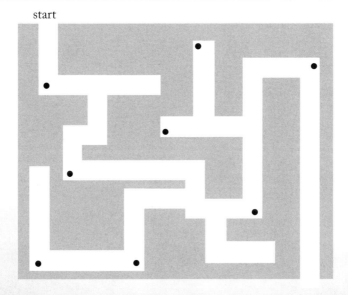

Discuss the following questions with your partner.
• Read your list of barriers to your partner. Which barrier on your list bothers you the most? What can you do about it?

• In what ways are you good and not-so-good at following through with your good intentions?

• What's one thing in your present lifestyle you would like to change that might help you be more like Timothy, showing genuine interest in others and following through with good intentions?

Rendezvous and Beyond 🚲

Use these ideas to find joy in serving others in the following week.
   • Read Matthew 25:31-40.

> "But when the Son of Man comes in his glory, and all the angels with him, then he will sit upon his glorious throne. All the nations will be gathered in his presence, and he will separate the people as a shepherd separates the sheep from the goats. He will place the sheep at his right hand and the goats at his left.
>
> Then the King will say to those on his right, 'Come, you who are blessed by my Father, inherit the Kingdom prepared for you from the creation of the world. For I was hungry, and you fed me. I was thirsty, and you gave me a drink. I was a stranger, and you invited me into your home. I was naked, and you gave me clothing. I was sick, and you cared for me. I was in prison, and you visited me.'
>
> Then these righteous ones will reply, 'Lord, when did we ever see you hungry and feed you? Or thirsty and give you something to drink? Or a stranger and show you hospitality? Or naked and give you clothing? When did we ever see you sick or in prison and visit you?'
>
> And the King will say, 'I tell you the truth, when you did it to one of the least of these my brothers and sisters, you were doing it to me!'" ☞ Matthew 25:31-40

Experiment with this Scripture passage this week. Find someone who is really hungry, and bring them food. Or go visit someone in prison. Or buy a new outfit for someone who has very little. Or sit on the bedside of someone who is ill and read to them. Whatever you pick to do, *picture Jesus as the person you are serving.* After your service "experiment," write down your reflections about how it made you feel.

_____

_____

_____

_____

_____

_____

_____

_____

_____

_____

_____

_____

_____

"It is very possible that you will find human beings, surely very near you, needing affection and love...Who is that someone? That person is Jesus himself: Jesus who is hidden under the guise of suffering!"
—Mother Teresa

ᏜᏜ *Rendezvous for Two* ᏜᏜ

Have a rendezvous with God, just the two of you.

Spend time this week reflecting on joy in your own life. Ask God to help you take an honest look at whether or not you are a joyful person.

• When are you most joyful?

_____

_____

_____

_____

_____

• Where does your real joy come from?

_____

_____

_____

_____

• How can you relate to Paul's joy that comes from "pouring [his life] out like a liquid offering?"

_____

_____

_____

_____

❧ *Notes* ❧

 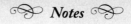

Joy Back and Forth

> "I want to know Christ and experience the mighty power that raised him from the dead. I want to suffer with him, sharing in his death, so that one way or another I will experience the resurrection from the dead!
>
> I don't mean to say that I have already achieved these things or that I have already reached perfection. But I press on to possess that perfection for which Christ Jesus first possessed me. No, dear brothers and sisters, I have not achieved it, but I focus on this one thing: Forgetting the past and looking forward to what lies ahead, I press on to reach the end of the race and receive the heavenly prize for which God, through Christ Jesus, is calling us.
>
> Let all who are spiritually mature agree on these things. If you disagree on some point, I believe God will make it plain to you. But we must hold on to the progress we have already made.
>
> Dear brothers and sisters, pattern your lives after mine, and learn from those who follow our example."
>
> ☞ Philippians 3:10-17

Summarize some of the main ideas in this passage.

- _____

- _____

- _____

Nudge Questions

Forget

• Why is it so hard for us to forget the things in our past that we've already been forgiven for?

• When does your past haunt you the most?

• How can you *actively forget* the things God doesn't want you to keep holding onto?

• If there's something God has forgiven you for, and you think he wants *you* to forget it too, write down here what it is and what you're going to do to let it go.

_____

_____

_____

_____

_____

_____

_____

_____

_____

_____

_____

_____

_____

Nudge Questions

Focus

• How does focusing on our future—being with God in heaven—help you find joy right now, in daily life?

• How can you make sure to focus on this target each day?

• Write here one thing you can do to focus each day on your future with Christ.

_____

_____

_____

_____

_____

_____

_____

> I want to be where you are,
> Dwelling in your presence
> Feasting at your table,
> Surrounded by your glory.
> —from "I Want to be Where You Are" by Don Moen

Rendezvous and Beyond

Use these ideas to keep focusing on God in the following week.
  • Write this translation of Philippians 3:10 on a few note cards and
  strategically place them in areas where you'll see them often this week.

> "[For my determined purpose is] that I may know Him
> (that I may progressively become more deeply and intimately
> acquainted with Him, perceiving and recognizing and
> understanding the wonders of His Person more strongly and
> more clearly)." ☞ Philippians 3:10, The Amplified Bible

Whom do you *know* really well? Think for a minute about this friendship.
How did you get to *know* them?

_____

_____

_____

_____

_____

How well do you feel like you *know* God?

_____

_____

_____

_____

  • Make this your prayer throughout the week: *Lord, I want to become more
  deeply and intimately acquainted with you. I need your Spirit to move in my
  heart. Even when I don't act like I care about you, move me closer to you, Lord.
  That is my deepest desire.*

• Do a word study of the word "know" in Philippians 3:10. To do this, you'll need some study tools, either online (try www.biblegateway.com or www.crosswalk.com) or actual books: Use Bible concordances, Bible dictionaries, Greek dictionaries, and topical word study books.

Here's a first step to get you started. The word translated "know" is "ginosko" in the Greek language. Find the meaning of that word in the dictionaries. Now, look up every verse that has this word in the New Testament. Remember, you're not looking up the English word, "know," you're looking up the Greek word that is translated "know." By reading each of those verses and the context in which you find the verses with this Greek word, you'll have a richer understanding of this *big* word that is translated into the little word "know."

In the space below, write all of your notes, thoughts, and comments about the word "ginosko."

_____

_____

_____

_____

_____

_____

_____

_____

_____

• For extra reading, check out one of these fantastic books:
  Seeing and Savoring Jesus Christ by John Piper
  Intimate Moments with the Savior by Ken Gire
  The Knowledge of the Holy by A.W. Tozer
  Knowing God by J.I. Packer
  Invitation to Solitude and Silence by Ruth Haley Barton
  Experiencing the Depths of Jesus Christ by Jeanne Guyon
  Your God Is Too Safe by Mark Buchanan

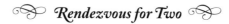

❧ *Rendezvous for Two* ❧

Have a rendezvous with God, just the two of you.

After doing your study of the word translated "know," reread Philippians 3:10a.

> **"I want to know Christ and experience the mighty power that raised him from the dead."** ☞ **Philippians 3:10a**

Reflect on any new insights and meanings the verse has for you.

_____

_____

_____

_____

_____

Pray this simple prayer when you wake up every morning:
Lord, I want to know you today.

• Try to stretch your mind, thinking outside the box as you seek to know God. Be open to knowing God in ways you may never have thought of before. Getting to know God doesn't have to be a deeply intellectual, theological exercise. It can be through simple, everyday things. It can involve simply noticing the wonder of God's creation around you—like when you watch a movie like *Charlotte's Web* and marvel at the intricacy of a spider web. Getting to know God can be as simple as watching a movie, seeing Charlotte make her web, and thinking, *Wow, God! You are amazing for coming up with that whole spider web design thing!*

Look for God in your everyday life. Seek to know his extraordinariness in the ordinariness around you. Spend time this week writing down what you experience.

Notes

The Peace-Joy Package

"Don't worry about anything; instead, pray about everything. Tell God what you need, and thank him for all he has done. Then you will experience God's peace, which exceeds anything we can understand. His peace will guard your hearts and minds as you live in Christ Jesus.

And now, dear brothers and sisters, one final thing. Fix your thoughts on what is true, and honorable, and right, and pure, and lovely, and admirable. Think about things that are excellent and worthy of praise. Keep putting into practice all you learned and received from me—everything you heard from me and saw me doing. Then the God of peace will be with you."

☞ Philippians 4:6-9

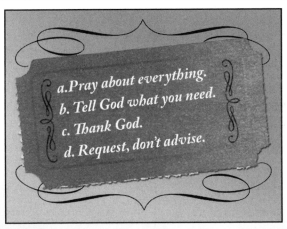

a. Pray about everything.
b. Tell God what you need.
c. Thank God.
d. Request, don't advise.

Nudge Questions

Worry Trade

• Why is it so easy to worry?

• What makes trusting God so difficult?

• In what area of your life would you like to have more peace?

• If God were to talk to you about your current worries, what do you think he'd say?

• Pair up and write down your partner's current worries:

a. personal worry: _____

b. family worry: _____

c. long-term, nagging worry: _____

Agree to pray each day in the next week for those worries to be lifted and for your partner to be able to truly trust God. Pray together now.

Fix Your Thoughts

> "And now, dear brothers and sisters, one final thing. Fix your thoughts on what is true, and honorable, and right, and pure, and lovely, and admirable. Think about things that are excellent and worthy of praise. Keep putting into practice all you learned and received from me—everything you heard from me and saw me doing. Then the God of peace will be with you."
> ☞ Philippians 4:8-9

Write down what you think God wants you to fix your thoughts on each day.

What is true?

_____

_____

_____

_____

What is right?

_____

_____

_____

What is pure?

_____

_____

_____

What is lovely?

_____

_____

_____

_____

What is admirable?

_____

_____

_____

_____

Rendezvous and Beyond

Use these ideas to keep growing in God's peace in the following week.
  • On the chart below, log your "Worry Activity" for one day.

The Worry	Number of Times I Worried	Result, If Known

1. How many times did you worry?

2. What percentage of your worries happened?

3. Of those worries that happened, were the results better or worse than expected?
  • On the chart below, list each worry from the above chart. Then, add the lie that is the premise behind the worry. (For example: The worry is "I'm never going to lose weight and look good." The lie behind that worry might be "I'm only valuable if I'm slim and attractive." Now, list the truth that opposes the lie. For example: "My value isn't based on looks. I'm a precious daughter of the King of kings!"

The Worry	The Lie	The Truth

• If you want to dig deeper into why we don't always focus on the truth, read a book about the lies we believe instead of the truth. A great book is Dr. Chris Thurman's *The Lies We Believe*.

• Do an informal survey: Interview friends this week, asking them what they think the perfect image of peace is. Record their answers below.

_____

_____

_____

_____

_____

_____

Do you notice a trend or pattern in their answers? If so, describe:

_____

_____

_____

_____

_____

Invite a few friends for lunch or for coffee, and throw out the following statement for discussion:
>   Peace isn't the absence of stress, it is…

_____

_____

_____

_____

❧ *Rendezvous for Two* ❧

Have a rendezvous with God, just the two of you.
  • Read Isaiah 26:3.

> **"You will keep in perfect peace all who trust in you, all whose thoughts are fixed on you!"** ☞ **Isaiah 26:3**

1. Write down what **perfect peace** would look like in your life.

_____

2. How does keeping your eyes fixed on God affect your peace?

_____

3. How does your level of peace impact your level of joy? Journal about what your joy level is like when you have peace and when you don't.

_____

_____

_____

_____

• Make a date with God this week for at least 30 minutes to walk through all of these four prayer steps:
a. Pray about everything. Just let your mind go, and whatever comes to mind, pray about it!

b. Tell God what you need. Don't hold back. All of your needs, even those you don't want to even think about, tell God about them.

c. Thank God. Thank him for the big things and the little things. Be creative!

d. Request, don't advise. Just ask. Say, "Here, God is _____. Please help! I need you."